**A Closer Look at
AMAZONIAN
INDIANS**

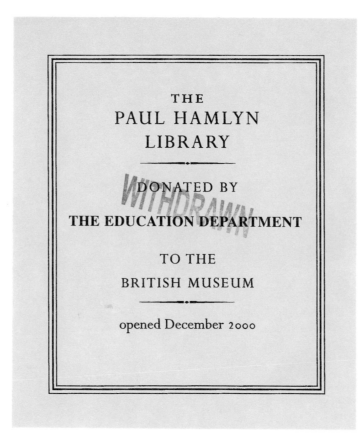

A CLOSER LOOK BOOK
© The Archon Press Ltd
1978

Originated and designed by
Charles Matheson, David Cook
Assoc., produced by
The Archon Press Ltd
70 Old Compton Street
London W1V 5PA

Dr. S. Hugh-Jones is a Lecturer in
Social Anthropology at Cambridge
University, and Fellow of Kings
College, Cambridge.
The publishers would like to
acknowledge the Dept. of
Ethnography at the British
Museum for providing access to
the Tayler/Moser collection.

First published in
Great Britain 1978 by
Hamish Hamilton
Children's Books Ltd
90 Great Russell Street
London WC1B 3PT

0 241 10049 6

Printed in Great Britain by
W. S. Cowell Ltd
Butter Market, Ipswich

# A closer LOOK at AMAZONIAN INDIANS

Stephen Hugh-Jones

Illustrated by
Maurice Wilson

Hamish Hamilton · London

# Indians of the Vaupés

**Barasana woman**
The native peoples of the Americas came originally from Asia. Some Barasana faces show this Mongoloid ancestry. In the past men and women wore long hair but now men crop theirs in European fashion. Women wear their hair in buns and use plastic combs obtained by trade. To emphasise their dark hair they outline the face and hairline with black paint made from leaves. Chilli peppers rubbed on the face build up a layer of grease as a base for red face paint – this adds beauty and is a sign of sociability. Small glass bead necklaces are valuable items of trade.

The Vaupés region lies near the Equator on the border of Colombia and Brazil; the River Vaupés, rising close to the Andes, flows east to join the Rio Negro, a tributary of the Amazon. The land is covered with thick tropical forest, an endless sea of green with bright patches of colour made by the tops of flowering trees. Breaking through the trees like islands are steep-sided, flat-topped mountains. The rivers cutting through these outcrops are blocked by falls and dangerous rapids.

In clearings on the banks of rivers live some fifteen thousand Amazonian Indians who make their living by hunting, fishing and agriculture. The Indians are divided into many small groups, each speaking its own language. Though the groups have names like the Tukano, Cubeo, Desana and Barasana, they are not really independent tribes; each group intermarries with its neighbours, shares a common culture and way of life. All the group languages belong to a common family called Tukanoan. Legends of the Vaupés Indians suggest they came from the east, but strange carvings on the rocks indicate that they have been in the region for a long time.

At the beginning of the century, the world became hungry for rubber to make tyres for the newly-developed motor car. The Vaupés is rich in rubber trees and the Indians were set to work collecting the rubber. They were paid little or nothing and many died from new diseases introduced by white settlers. The rubber gatherers were followed by missionaries who ordered the Indians to move from their traditional houses, or *malocas*, into villages. This book is about the traditional way of life of the Vaupés Indians, represented by the Barasana, a small group living on the River Pirá-Paraná. The Barasana and their neighbours, protected by their dangerous and isolated river, escaped the worst effects of the rubber trade and early missionary efforts.

## Amazonia

Amazonia's world position is shown above. Below is the general region, centred on the Amazon and its tributaries, showing the location of Indian tribes.

CUBEO

BARASANA

R. Piró-Paraná

R. Vaupés

DESANA

TUKANO

0    100 km.

R. Amazon

5

# A forest clearing

**People of the Pirá-Paraná**
Groups have traditional territories. The Tatuyo live in the headwater region, the Makuna towards the river mouth, the Barasana across the middle, flanked by the Taiwano and Bará.

The Barasana have no villages; instead, small groups of people live in malocas (communal houses), each one separated from its neighbours by about an hour's journey. People in nearby malocas visit each other often, attending dances and intermarrying. More distant people are rarely visited and often regarded with suspicion. Indians prefer to build malocas close to the bigger rivers where fishing is good and travel easy. During the rubber boom, they moved up on to small streams hidden in the forest; today, with peace established, they are moving down again.

From the air, the large gardens or *chagras* around the malocas look like light green holes in the forest. Each maloca is surrounded by a cleared space or plaza. Behind the house are smaller gardens for special plants: tobacco, medicines and drugs, peppers for cooking. Banana trees round the plaza provide fruit and their leaves are used for serving food.

As a group the Barasana number about 300 and other groups are roughly the same size. The groups are descended from different mythical ancestors – all anacondas (huge water snakes). Barasana men and women must marry partners from other groups: Tatuyo, Taiwano, Makuna or Bará. Groups are divided into clans which are ranked in order; clans refer to those above them as 'older brothers' and to those below as 'younger brothers'.

Ideally the members of one clan should live in the same maloca; though this rarely happens, malocas of the same clan are often built close to one another. Between five and thirty people live in a maloca. The men of the house are usually brothers and the women are their wives and unmarried sisters. On marriage, sisters leave the house and join their husbands in other malocas. When adult men die, the maloca is often abandoned, the community moving together to a new site close by. As the men grow older, and their sons grow up and marry, the household gets bigger. When the last of the senior generation dies, the house is abandoned and the community splits up with the male children founding new malocas of their own in new locations.

## Looking after the maloca

Smoke from the fires inside preserves the palm leaf thatch but the hot sun and rain slowly rot it away. Men collect new leaves in the forest, bring them back to the plaza and weave them onto strips of wood. The sections of thatch are put in place from a scaffold constructed inside the house. Malocas are built as large as possible so as to hold plenty of visitors and to leave space for dancing; big malocas are called *basaria wi*, 'dance houses'. The size, state of repair and cleanliness of the maloca reflect on the inhabitants' prestige. The area round the maloca is kept free from weeds. Paths radiate out – one from the front door to the port on the main river; another leads from the back to a stream and on to the gardens; still more lead to hunting territories and to other malocas. The front wall of the maloca is brightly painted.

# The maloca

A maloca may last up to fifteen years before it no longer
becomes worthwhile to repair it. To build a new one can take more
than a year. All housebuilding is done by men, using materials
gathered in the forest. Most of the work is done by the men who
will live in the house but they may be helped by their neighbours.
One of them, usually the eldest brother, directs the work and he
will later become the headman of the maloca. The biggest malocas
are up to a hundred feet long; the larger the maloca and the more
people living in it, the greater the headman's prestige.

After clearing the ground of roots and stumps, a plan of the
house is traced in the sand. Two rows of centre posts, made from
hardwood and sunk deep in the earth, are erected first, followed
by smaller side posts. The ridgepole rests on small uprights lashed
to the central beam running the length of the house. Other
horizontal beams, supported by the cross-ties and side posts,
carry long thin poles running from the ridge down nearly to the
ground at either side. When the framework is completed, the men
go to the forest to collect roofing leaves, returning with huge,
heavy bundles on their backs. They weave the leaves into a dense
thatch, different men using their own weaving styles. As soon as

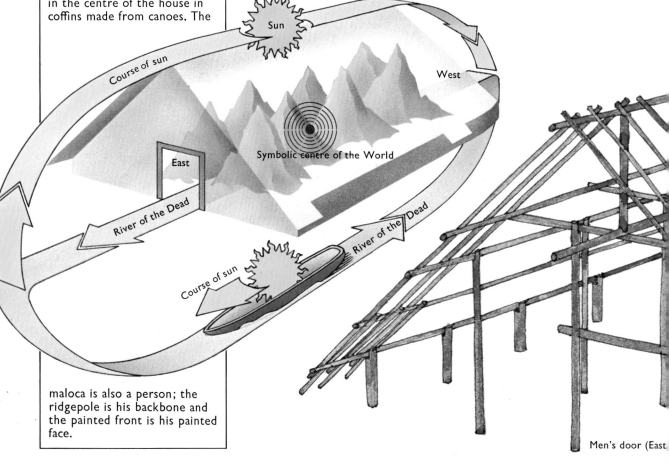

Course of sun

Sun

West

Symbolic centre of the World

East

River of the Dead

River of the Dead

Course of sun

Men's door (East

one section of the roof is complete, the household, who have been camping in shelters nearby, move into their new home.

When all the walls are closed and the sheets of flattened bark on the front have been painted, a big dance is held to celebrate the end of the work and to reward the people who helped. The dance is a festive occasion attended by people from all the neighbouring malocas. During the dance, the shamans (who can communicate with the spirit world) chant and blow spells to make the house strong, to protect it from thunder and lightning and to keep the inhabitants safe from misfortune.

For the Barasana, their maloca is the centre of their world and their life. It serves as a family home, a workshop, a meeting place, a dance hall, a church and represents the universe itself. Every married man makes himself a screened off compartment along the side walls towards the rear of the maloca where he will live with his wife and children. Unmarried men and any visitors sleep in the open area towards the front. The back of the maloca serves as a kitchen area and in some houses a rounded end is added at the rear to provide more room for the preparation and cooking of manioc bread.

**Lashing**
The framework of the maloca is lashed together with vines. The shamans blow spells over them when the house is ready, to prevent them from loosening.

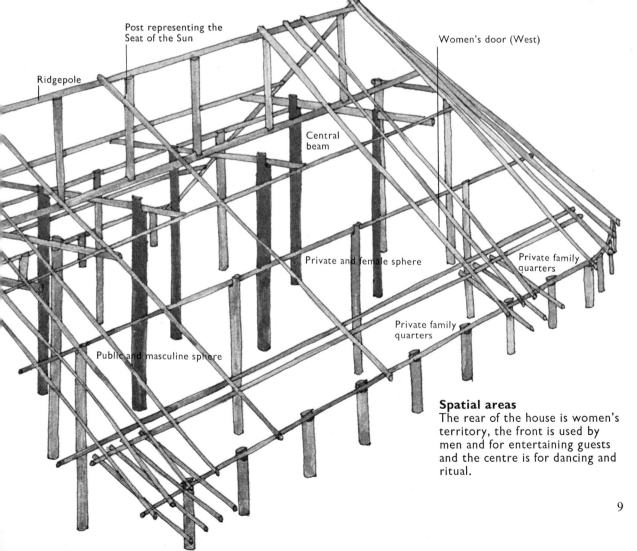

Post representing the Seat of the Sun

Women's door (West)

Ridgepole

Central beam

Private and female sphere

Private family quarters

Private family quarters

Public and masculine sphere

**Spatial areas**
The rear of the house is women's territory, the front is used by men and for entertaining guests and the centre is for dancing and ritual.

9

# Inside

## Life in the maloca

The Barasana get up very early and go to the river to bathe. The Indians are very clean and bathe often. Breakfast is a light meal, usually of manioc bread dipped in a hot sauce made from manioc, peppers and fish scraps. Men provide meat and fish for the family and women provide manioc (a root from which tapioca is made). Meat or fish must always be eaten with manioc – this represents the unity of men and women.

After breakfast people go off to work. Women go to the chagras and some of the men leave to hunt or fish while others stay behind to work in the house. Men and women make different things. Men weave baskets, make weapons and fishing gear, carve stools from blocks of wood, make the big troughs which hold manioc beer, the wicker stands for pots and gourds and the long, hollow tube tied to the housepost which is for sieving coca (a plant which is used as a stimulant). Maize, grown by men, is stored in the rafters. Dance ornaments made by them are hung in a palm leaf box from a beam above the coca tube. Women make pottery, sew clothes, weave hammocks and the garters worn below the knees, make body paint and do almost all the cooking and agricultural work. Clothes, steel axes and machetes, metal cooking pots and wooden trunks are traded from white people. The women rear small animals orphaned in the hunt and young birds as pets. Chickens are treated as pets and never eaten. Macaws are kept for their feathers. After plucking, their skins are rubbed with a special fruit. Their feathers grow bright orange and are used for feather crowns. Dusk is a time for family life when men play with their children. At night, men sit together telling stories, chewing coca and smoking cigars. The women sit towards the back, going away to sleep in their hammocks before the men.

# Farming the forest

To make their chagras or gardens, the Indians clear patches of forest near the maloca, burn the tree stumps and plant their crops in the ashes. When the crops have been harvested, a chagra is abandoned and slowly turns back into forest. The forest cover restores fertility to the soil so that after about fifteen years the old site can be cleared and used again. This kind of farming is called 'slash and burn' and is practised by Indians and white people throughout Amazonia.

Many different crops are grown together in one chagra; plants of different heights provide shade for one another and their leaves act as a barrier to the heavy rain which otherwise would wash away the soil. Familiar crops like pineapples, tobacco, cashew nuts, peanuts and manioc were first cultivated by Amazonian Indians. The Barasana also grow bananas, plantains, sugar cane and yams which were introduced to the New World by European settlers. In addition to food crops, they grow arrow canes, vines to make fish poisons, leaves to make red and black body paints and medicines.

Apart from felling and burning the forest, the men do very little agricultural work and the chagras are looked after by the women. Every morning the women set off together to collect manioc to make the day's supply of manioc bread. They peel the heavy tubers and load them into baskets which are carried with a strip of bark over the forehead. The men contrast their destruction of the forest with the care the women take over their crops; they call the women 'food mothers' and compare the manioc to their children.

**Slash and burn** (below)
Chagras are made at the start of the dry season in December. Men clear the undergrowth, fell trees and in February, just before the rains begin, set fire to the dry branches and leaves. Women plant crops in the ashes. Men plant coca, maize, poison vines and *yagé* (from which a strong drink is made). The garden is weeded once and the manioc is ready for harvesting after about nine months. The manioc is finished as a crop after three years and weeds begin to take over the garden but coca and bananas continue to be harvested. A new chagra is cleared every year so that there is always one ready to harvest:
1. Maloca
2. Clearing and burning the forest
3. Newly-planted chagra
4. Chagra ready for harvesting
5. Almost abandoned chagra with fruit trees and encroaching jungle
6. Totally abandoned chagra with newer forest trees

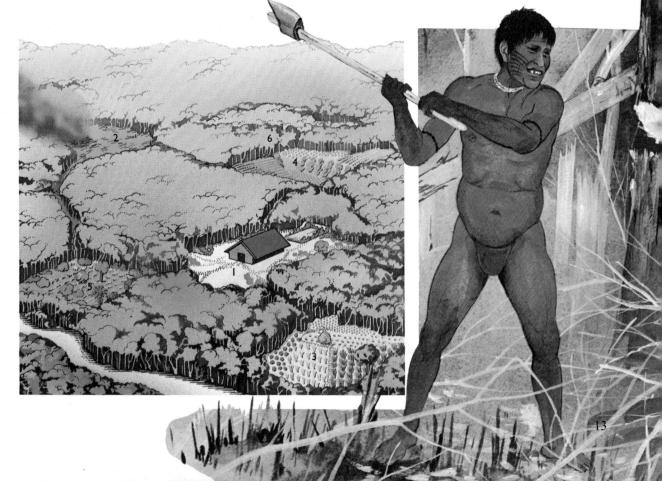

# The women's world

The lives of Barasana men and women are sharply divided. Inside the maloca they use different doors and carry out their separate tasks in different areas. Outside, women work in the gardens, men in the forest and on the rivers.

The world of women revolves round the care of children, growing crops and preparing manioc and other food. The process required to turn manioc into food is lengthy and time-consuming but the root does produce a good crop in poor soil and many different foods can be made from it. The leaves are eaten as spinach. The boiled juice makes a drink (*manicuera*); boiled longer it makes a caramel-flavoured sauce. The grated roots make many kinds of bread. Toasted bread, mixed with boiled juice and allowed to ferment, makes the beer drunk at dances. Manioc pulp toasted dry makes nutty granules (*farinha*) which keep for long periods and can be carried on journeys.

As women process manioc, they put their babies in special slings (like baby bouncers) hung from the roof: when a baby walks his feet leave the ground and he swings back out of harm's way. Not every woman knows how to make all the manioc dishes, how to weave and make pottery and how to grow all the different crops. Those who do are much admired.

As a rest from working manioc, women and children sometimes go off to the forest on expeditions called 'looking and eating'. They collect ants, frogs and caterpillars, fish in the streams for crabs and shrimps and chop down fruit trees with axes. They eat what they can in the forest, bringing the rest back to cook at home. Men also take their wives and children for holidays, camping in shelters on the river banks to catch fish or eat fruit in season. And sometimes the whole household goes off to live in shelters and gather food.

**Pottery**
This is made by women using clay from the banks of streams. The clay is mixed with ash to make it stronger. The pots are built by coiling and the sides smoothed with a piece of gourd. The dried surface is polished with a pebble and, after firing, the pots are coated with leaf juice and smoked to give a black glaze. Most pots have round bottoms which stand firm on the sandy house floor.

**Manioc processing** (*left, right*)
Manioc (1) contains prussic acid which must be removed before it can be eaten. The tubers are grated on a board (2) set with stone chips and the pulp put into a sieve on a tripod (3). Water is poured on it, washing juice mixed with starch into a pot below. The juice is poured off and boiled to get rid of the poison, making a pleasant drink. Before the pulp is mixed with starch and placed on a dish to be baked as manioc bread (4), it is put into a *tipiti* (5) hanging from a pole. A woman sits on another pole going through the loop at the bottom. Her weight squeezes the tipiti, forcing the liquid out which flows through the sides.

15

# Life on the river

The Barasana and their neighbours are very much 'river people'; they build their houses by rapids where fish are plentiful, prefer to travel by canoe and obtain much of their food from rivers. They believe that the first people came up-river from the east and today rivers for them represent a continuing connection with the source of life.

Canoe-making is a highly skilled activity and only some men know how to do it. Canoes are valuable trading items. The Indians are expert canoemen and have a detailed knowledge of ways through the dangerous rapids that block the rivers. Different sizes of canoe are used for various purposes, large ones for carrying people and goods over long distances and small ones, just big enough for a single person, for hunting and fishing. The Indians hunt from canoes at night using torches and firing at the eyes of caimans and other animals reflected in their beams.

The Indians know exactly where to find different kinds of fish, what food they eat and what kind of bait they will take. In addition to hooks and line, fish are trapped at the mouths of streams and in the flooded forest, shot with bows and arrows, speared with harpoons and even chopped in half with machetes as they swim in the shallow water.

**Shooting fish**
To shoot fish, allowance has to be made for the bending of light; the man must aim at the fish itself not where it appears to be. The arrow's hollow shaft floats in the water; the end is tipped with a point and a bone or metal barb.

**Trapping fish**
The Indians build a dam across the river and set conical traps in it. They trample poison vines into the water, stunning the fish which are then caught in the traps or harpooned.

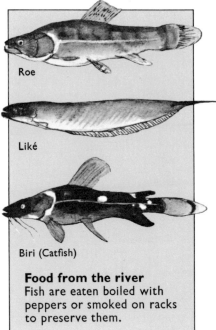

Roe

Liké

Biri (Catfish)

**Food from the river**
Fish are eaten boiled with peppers or smoked on racks to preserve them.

**Making canoes**
Dugout canoes are shaped from tree trunks. The inside is hollowed out with a large chisel from a slit running along the top. The canoe is heated and burned over a fire to make it pliable, the sides pulled apart with wooden pegs and kept open by the seats which are forced into place. Charring prevents the wood from rotting. Some Indians of Amazonia make bark canoes, like the North American Indians, but the Barasana use the whole trunk of a very large tree.

# Food from the forest

There is a very large number of different animal species in the Amazon rain forest but they are thinly distributed. To hunt them successfully requires an intimate knowledge of their habits and ways of life and an ability to interpret tracks, broken branches, fallen fruit and other signs of their presence. Hunting is done exclusively by men and good hunters acquire considerable respect and prestige. Though fish is eaten more than meat, hunting is the focus of interest for Barasana men. Stories of past hunts and recent sightings of animals dominate their conversation.

Men usually hunt alone or in pairs, often accompanied by dogs. Good hunting dogs are highly valued. Shotguns, obtained through trade with rubber gatherers or by work on mission stations, have largely replaced the traditional bows and arrows and their use has seriously depleted the animal population. Blowpipes are still used to hunt birds and monkeys because their silent darts do not scare away the game. Hunters usually set out in the morning, returning late in the afternoon. They go after specific animals but will take anything they come across. Tapirs are killed when asleep at mid-day or surprised at salt licks at night. Armadillos are driven from their holes with smoke. By imitating their calls, the Indians can bring many kinds of animals and birds within range.

As hunters walk through the forest, they are continually on the lookout for useful raw materials and for food that can be gathered. In the rainy season, large quantities of forest fruits are collected and form the focus of important ceremonies. Ants, caterpillars, frogs and grubs that live in the trunks of palm trees are all eaten and probably supply essential minerals and vitamins. Smoked meat and fish and other forest products are stored and then exchanged with other malocas during dances.

**Hunting weapons**
Blowpipes are made from two hollow palm wood tubes one inside the other, with a hardwood mouthpiece. Darts and hunting arrows are tipped with curare poison traded from neighbours.

Blowpipe

Dart

Outer tube

Hardwood mouthpiece

Quiver for darts

Bow and arrows

Section through pipe showing inner tube

## Favoured victims

**Woolly monkey**
Monkeys are called by making sucking noises in cupped hands and are shot with blowpipes.

**Toucan**
Hunters imitate the birds' call. Their meat is eaten and the feathers are used for ornaments.

**Peccary**
Peccaries are shot for their meat with arrows or guns or are trapped in hollow logs.

# Family life

Men marry women from other malocas who speak different languages from their own. Children are taught to speak their father's language but know their mother's perfectly too. Adults always speak in their own language but as they also know up to five others, they have no difficulty in understanding each other.

On marriage, a young man builds himself a compartment inside the maloca. When his wife has a child, he must stay with her in the compartment for ten days fasting and avoiding work. When babies are weaned, they spend much of their time playing with other children of the maloca who form a play group. Older children, especially older sisters, are expected to look after younger ones. Children do not go to school but learn by playing together, watching their parents and working with them. By the time they are six, young girls begin to help their mothers. Boys lead a freer life, swimming in the rivers and practising hunting with miniature bows and arrows or blowpipes. Later they begin to hunt and fish more seriously, bringing small birds and fish to their mothers to cook.

During the day, families may go inside their compartments in the maloca for peace and privacy. When men bring in fish or meat it is taken into the compartment and the family may have a small meal together before taking the pot out for the rest of the house. Supplies of fish and meat are kept on a rack hanging above the fire; the smoke and heat dry out the meat and preserve it. Clothes are hung from the rafters and women keep their best pots and gourds inside their compartments. Men store treasures in wooden trunks and keep their fishing gear and weapons stuck in the thatch.

Women often go with their husbands and children to visit their parents and brothers in neighbouring malocas; their husbands usually take along gifts of food or basketry to give to their in-laws. At sunrise and dusk, men sit out on the plaza talking with their wives and playing with their children, a family time that contrasts with their separation for the rest of the day.

**Sleeping in hammocks**
The family sleep in hammocks inside their compartment. Hammocks are still made from string twisted out of palm leaf fibre but the Indians prefer cotton hammocks bought from traders and missionaries.

# A man's life

**Coca**
Coca chewing wards off hunger and sleep and is an important social activity among the men.

**Toasting and pounding**
The coca leaves are toasted in a pot, pounded in a mortar, mixed with leaf ash and sieved.

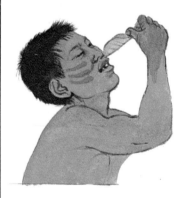

**Chilli pepper juice**
Juice from crushed peppers is inhaled as a physical and spiritual purge.

In the old days, before white people arrived, the Barasana were brave warriors. They say they were like the jaguar, the fiercest animal in the forest. They fought with strangers in distant malocas, capturing their women and their ritual possessions. Later, they fought the rubber gatherers who came to force them to work. Today there is no more war but the ideals of strength and courage live on. Men who act tough and talk hard are much admired.

During initiation, young men are whipped and given magical substances to eat to make them hard and strong. They bathe before dawn, thumping the water with their hands and drinking water which they vomit up to clean out their insides. They decorate their bodies with beads and paint and show off their skills in the manly pursuits of hunting, chopping down trees, paddling canoes and dancing. Before marriage they travel to other malocas to attend dances and go to mission stations and trading posts to work.

After marriage, men settle down. They make gardens for their wives, hunt and fish to feed their families and spend much of their time growing and processing coca. Every night, the men sit on stools in the middle of the house discussing the day's events. The headman encourages his brothers to work together and acts as their spokesman but he cannot give them orders.

Beyond the maloca, in the forest, live animals, spirits and other people. The outside world is a man's world. The crops they grow – coca, tobacco and maize for making beer – are all used during rituals when outsiders come to dance and when the men make contact with spirits. Hardworking men who are good hunters and who entertain many visitors earn respect and importance. They try to make their gardens as big as possible so that they will have plenty of manioc to make beer and plenty of coca to give their guests.

**Baskets**
These are used by women but only men may make them. Young men are taught to make sieves, trays and carrying baskets as part of their initiation.

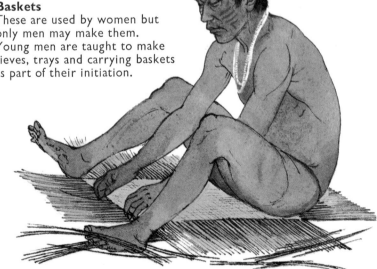

### Initiation
When boys approach adolescence, they go through an initiation rite. They are shown sacred flutes and trumpets representing the first ancestors. Women and children never see these. As the adults play the flutes, the young men are given yagé to drink which allows them to see visions of the spirit world. They are whipped by the shamans to make them brave.

**Curing illness**
A shaman sits his patient down.
He rubs his hands over the
affected part then sucks hard,
pulling spines or animal fur from
his mouth which he says have
caused the trouble.

# Myth, magic and medicine

The Indians' religion is based on myths or stories about the beginning of time which they believe to be true. They say that the sun made the world in the form of a big maloca. In the beginning there were no people. The first ancestors, the sun's children, came into the world through the front door in the east and swam up-river in the form of anacondas. As they travelled, they stopped at the rapids on the way to dance and sing. Carved on the rocks in the rivers there are men and spirits and even human footprints said to have been left there by the first people.

When they got to the middle of the earth, the Pirá-Paraná region, the anacondas stopped and turned into people. Each anaconda made people of a different language. The head became the top clan, the neck came next and so on down to the tail which became the most junior clan of all. These first people had names like Tapir, Jaguar, Armadillo and Deer, the names of the animals in the forest. In the beginning people and animals were like each other and lived in the same way. But as men got hold of fire to cook and to burn the forest, as they learned to make gardens and build houses and live together in society, they became different.

When the first people died, their bones are said to have turned into the sacred trumpets shown to boys at initiation rites. But their souls lived on and became spirit animals in the forest. Today, too, when people die, their souls return to the spirit world and join the animals and ancestors in the forest. Dead people go to the underworld river and float down to the west. Their souls return as babies who take the names of dead grandparents.

Mothers have their babies outside the maloca in the gardens and bring them in through the back door, the door in the west. When someone dies, the people are sad at their loss but the spirits are glad at their gain. When a baby is born, it is the spirits who lose and the people who gain. The spirits are jealous and try to get back their friend. The shaman must do magic to protect the newborn baby from the spirits who try to kill him. In the old days, when a person died, a ceremony was held at which the men wore masks representing all the animals in the forest. These were the spirit animals welcoming the soul of the dead man back into their world. So people and animals go round and round, from life to death and back again and from maloca to forest and back again.

Because animals and people were the same in the past and because animals and spirits live together today, when men go hunting it is as if they were going to war. When animals are killed in the hunt, their spirits try to take revenge. Through their meat, which is eaten as food, they send magical darts and other harmful things into the bodies of the hunter and his family. Most illnesses are believed to be caused in this way. Shamans are asked to blow spells over meat to send away the spirits and make it safe to eat. The shamans are the masters of the spirits. When they die, shamans' souls become jaguars, the masters of the animal world. The shaman acts as master of ceremonies at dances, allowing others to contact the spirits, protecting them from harm.

**Rock engravings**
Carved into rocks in the Pirá-Paraná are strange figures and patterns. Some say that these were made by the first ancestors when they paused in their journey up-river from the door in the east. There are other stories, too, about the carvings, which are etched about half an inch into the rock face. Directly above is one which may represent the river god, Ní. The rock on which he is carved was once a pile of manioc, placed there by the people. Ní turned it to stone and now he sits in his palace, the underwater cave below the rapids, singing to the drawings and the spirits.

# Gathering together

Indians travel a great deal and rely on each other for hospitality. It is rare to spend a week in a maloca without someone coming to stay or passing through. The Indians go to visit relatives, to trade or to seek help for work or when people are ill. But when they invite guests to their own maloca, it is always to dance and to drink beer. Dances are held throughout the year. There are many different kinds of ritual festival. At some, guests bring huge quantities of smoked fish and meat. At others, men bring baskets of forest fruits into the house to the sound of the sacred trumpets. Dances are held to celebrate the end of initiation, the end of garden clearing and other important occasions.

On the day before a dance, women gather piles of manioc and other roots from the chagras. The boiled roots and toasted manioc bread are chewed then put in a trough with boiled manioc juice and left to ferment into beer. Men pick baskets of coca leaves, spending the rest of the day making them into powder. The house is swept clean and the earth floor sprinkled with water to keep down the dust. An air of excitement hangs over the maloca. The young men practise their panpipes and the elders get ready the feather headdresses, maracas and other items used in the dance.

Dances are important social events to people living in isolated malocas in the forest. A house full of guests is like a village. Dances serve many purposes: they are religious rituals, a time for amusement, an opportunity to swap news, to renew old contacts and to make new friends.

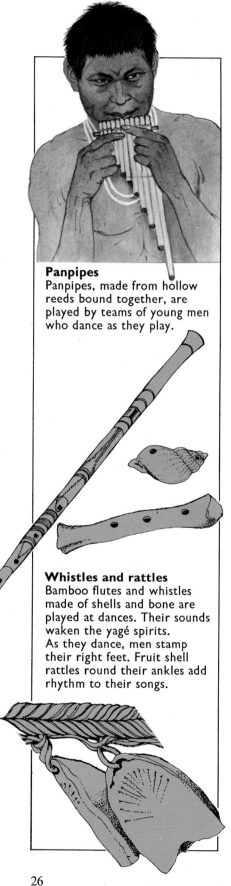

### Panpipes
Panpipes, made from hollow reeds bound together, are played by teams of young men who dance as they play.

### Whistles and rattles
Bamboo flutes and whistles made of shells and bone are played at dances. Their sounds waken the yagé spirits.
As they dance, men stamp their right feet. Fruit shell rattles round their ankles add rhythm to their songs.

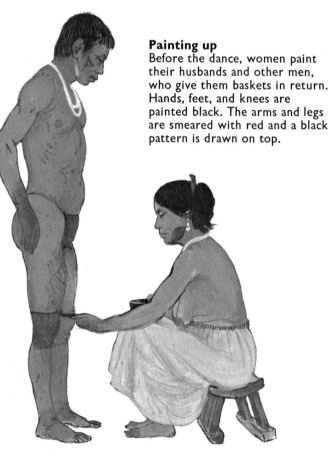

### Painting up
Before the dance, women paint their husbands and other men, who give them baskets in return. Hands, feet, and knees are painted black. The arms and legs are smeared with red and a black pattern is drawn on top.

## Full regalia

Ritual ornaments have magic power and only adult men may wear them. They are the dress of spirits and ancestors. A fully-dressed dancer wears a macaw-feather crown, trimmed with down with an egret plume behind. Round his neck is a quartz pendant. His belt is of ocelot or peccary teeth. At the front he has a painted bark-cloth apron and sweet-smelling herbs are tucked under his belt at the back. Below his knees are woven garters and he wears a rattle on one ankle and a band of white bark on the other. Different instruments are used for different dances: balsa wood thumping tubes when food is exchanged, maracas when fruit is gathered.

### Yagé pot

Yagé is made from the bark of a cultivated vine, pounded and mixed with water. The bitter liquid, served at dances, gives men visions of the spirit world. The yagé is put into painted pots, decorated with scenes from yagé visions. Pots full of yagé are left out in the sun to ferment.

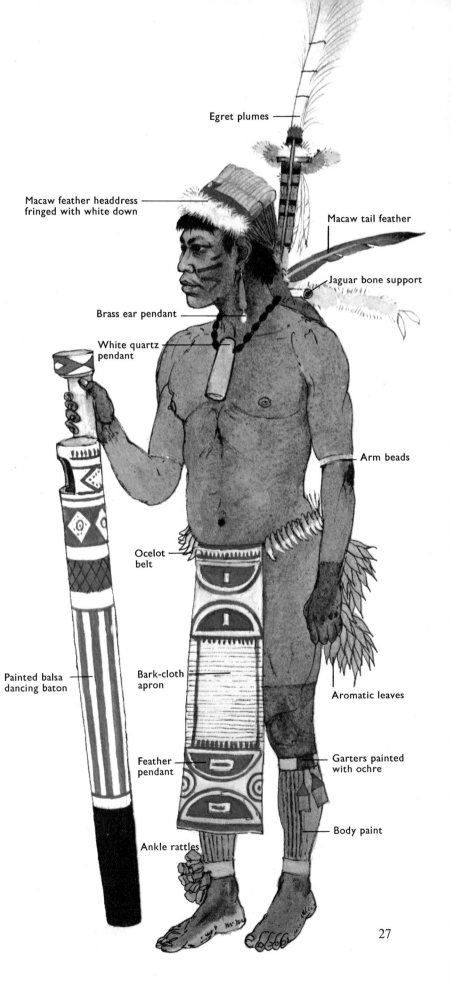

Egret plumes

Macaw feather headdress fringed with white down

Macaw tail feather

Jaguar bone support

Brass ear pendant

White quartz pendant

Arm beads

Ocelot belt

Bark-cloth apron

Aromatic leaves

Painted balsa dancing baton

Feather pendant

Garters painted with ochre

Ankle rattles

Body paint

27

# Drinking and dancing

Dances usually start in the morning and continue without a break until the next day. The night is a sacred time. The guests arrive by canoe or by trail, stopping at the river to bathe and decorate themselves. The men go in at the front of the house, chanting loud greetings to their hosts. The women, loaded down with baskets and babies on their hips, go in at the back.

At first the atmosphere is restrained and formal but as the day wears on, the air is filled with chatter and hoots of laughter. The visitors are served with gourds of beer which they must drain in one go. They are shamed if they cannot empty the trough by morning. After the greetings, men prepare for dancing, putting on their headdresses and ornaments and shaking rattles and maracas in anticipation. As one group dances in line, panpipes are played in chorus from the sidelines. The young men spring up, weaving in and out of the houseposts, playing their pipes and taking girls by the hand to dance.

When there is a break in the dancing, the men sit down on stools and the shaman hands them gourds of yagé with beer to take away the bitter taste. The men sit in a circle chanting the myths of their ancestors and how they came from the east to people the land. In their yagé visions, the men see the maloca as the universe, filled with ancestral spirits dressed in feathers and paint.

At the end of the dance everyone is exhausted but happy. The shaman removes the men's headdresses, blowing spells to protect them from the danger of wearing sacred things. The people go down to the river to bathe then back to their hammocks to sleep through the day. At dusk a big meal is served, the first one since the dancing began, and everyone eats hungrily. The next day, the visitors drift home carrying presents of food from their relatives and beads and other goods traded with the people they met.

# An uncertain future

Unlike some of the other tribes of Amazonia, the Indians of the Vaupés are not threatened with extinction but the traditional culture of the Barasana, described here, has largely disappeared from the rest of the Vaupés region. The malocas have gone and with them the spiritual values that gave meaning to life in the forest. Most Vaupés Indians now live in villages on the river banks, clustered around the mission stations. Each family has its own house with clay walls and a thatched roof.

With many people living in the same place for long periods, the resources of the forest become exhausted. Each year new gardens are cut where old ones were made not long ago. The soil, burned by the sun and washed out by the rain, becomes sterile and hard. The animals in the forest have been hunted out and few fish remain in the rivers. On the Pirá-Paraná there is still plenty to eat but elsewhere the diet is poor.

The rubber industry has almost collapsed; synthetic rubber is cheaper to produce. The hunting of jaguars for their skins has been outlawed. The few white people find it hard to make a living; Indians find it even harder – selling fruit and vegetables in the towns and working as casual labourers. New roads are being built into the region from Brazil which could allow the Indians to sell their produce and handicrafts in the distant cities but they also pose a problem. With improved communication, settlers may arrive, taking away the land and cutting down the forest on which the Indians' lives depend.

Indians living on the mission stations get good education but this, too, brings problems. Children go to boarding schools at a time when they would otherwise be learning to make a living from the forest and being taught their own culture by their parents. Instead, they learn about the outside world, about towns and cities and the possessions of white people. They would like to play a part in the life of Colombia and Brazil but at the moment they cannot do so. They go back to their homes unsuited to the old life and cut off from the new one.

It is easy to see the problems facing the Indians but less easy to find solutions. If the Indians were given rights to the lands they have occupied for hundreds of years, this at least would allow them to go on feeding themselves. But this would not be enough. The Indians depend on white people for steel axes and machetes and their life would now be impossible without them. They need to work to earn money to buy these and other goods. Uranium, which has recently been discovered in the Vaupés region, could bring in money, but unless things change, is unlikely to benefit the Indians.

The Indians of the Vaupés have known change for at least a hundred years. They have adapted to the presence of white people, they are open and curious about the outside world and welcome the opportunities and excitement it brings. But until they can find a better place in Colombian and Brazilian society, their future remains uncertain.

# Index